Debt Free Life

Lina Hernandez

Lina Hernandez

Copyright Page

Legal and Rights Data

Copyright Holder: © Lina Hernandez
Author: © Lina Hernandez 2025
Year: 2025
Country of the writer: Colombia

First Edition

Lina Hernandez

Index

The Invisible Weight of Debt

Debt is something that can creep into our lives almost without us realizing it. At first, it seems harmless, like a small favor we do for ourselves. Maybe it's a credit card purchase, a loan for something we really need, or just an expense we think we can cover later. But over time, debt grows. Not just in numbers, but in the weight it carries with it. And that weight, even if you don't see it, is always there.

It's like carrying a backpack that seems light at first, but with every step, every day, it gets heavier. You may not notice it right away, because you're used to it, because everyone around you seems to be carrying similar backpacks, too. Yet deep down, you know it's there, hampering your movements, making it harder for you to move forward. Debt, even when you're not thinking about it directly, affects the way you live, how you make decisions, and how you feel about yourself.

One of the first signs of debt burden is stress. You might be sitting at home watching TV or trying to enjoy a quiet moment, but suddenly, a thought invades your mind: that payment that's coming due, that balance that just keeps growing. It's like you can never fully switch off. You might not talk about it with anyone, you might try to ignore it, but you know it's there, like a shadow that follows you everywhere.

In addition to stress, debt also affects the way we perceive our future. When you have debt, it’s hard to think about long-term plans. The dream vacation, the house you want to buy, even something as simple as going out to dinner with friends, can feel like a luxury you can’t afford. Instead of looking forward with hope, you start to feel trapped, as if all your effort is going into putting out financial fires instead of building something meaningful.

The tricky thing about debt is that it doesn’t just affect your wallet, it affects your emotions as well. There’s a mix of guilt, shame, and frustration that can be hard to explain. Maybe you wonder how you got into this situation, what you could have done differently, or whether you’ll ever be able to get out of it. These emotions are heavy, and they can even affect your relationships. Maybe you avoid certain conversations with your partner or friends because you don't want them to know what you're going through. Maybe you feel less capable, less worthy, because debt has a way of making us feel like we've failed, even if we haven't.

The important thing here is to remember that you are not alone. Many people go through the same thing. Debt is a common reality, but it doesn't have to be a permanent fate. It's easy to fall into the trap of thinking that things will never get better, that the weight will always be there, but that's not true. The first thing you need to do is acknowledge it, admit that the weight exists, because only then can you start looking for a solution.

Imagine for a moment what your life would be like without that weight. Being able to take a deep breath without financial worries weighing you down. Making decisions without the pressure of debt pushing you in directions you don't want. Having the freedom to think about your dreams, your goals, without money being a constant barrier. That life is possible, but it starts here, with the recognition of what you're facing and the commitment to do something about it.

Don't blame yourself for being in this situation. Most debts are not a reflection of your worth as a person, but of decisions that seemed like the best options at the time. The key is to take control. Debt can feel like a huge, scary monster, but like any problem, it can be tackled step by step. Every small action you take, every conscious decision, is a brick you're removing from that wall that seems to be closing you in.

The weight of debt is real, but so is the possibility of breaking free from it. Remember that you are not defined by the money you owe. You are much more than that. This chapter is not only to show you that the weight exists, but also to tell you that you don't have to carry it forever. It can be left behind, and in this book you will find the tools to do so. The backpack you carry can become lighter, until one day you discover that it is no longer there. That day will come, and when it does, you will realize that all this effort was worth it.

Making Peace with Finances

When it comes to finances, most people have a complicated relationship with money. It's like a friend who is sometimes there to support you, but other times seems to cause more problems than it solves. For many, money is a constant source of stress, arguments, and worries. However, the truth is that money itself is not the problem. The problem is how we relate to it, how we understand it, and how we manage it. If you're reading this, it's probably because you feel like something in your relationship with money isn't working as it should. And that's okay, because acknowledging it is the first step to making peace with your finances.

Making peace with money doesn't mean you suddenly have everything figured out. It doesn't mean your debts will magically disappear or you'll start making more money. Rather, it's about changing the way you view and handle it. Money is often treated as an enemy, something that seems to slip through your fingers or that there's never enough of. But money has no emotions or intentions; it's simply a tool. Like any tool, it's up to you to learn how to use it correctly.

The first step to making peace with your finances is to accept where you are now. This can be uncomfortable, but it is necessary. If you are in debt, if you are spending more than you earn, or if you have no savings, you need to face it honestly. There is no point in beating yourself up for past decisions. What's done is done. The important thing is that today you have the opportunity to start over, to take control and build a healthier relationship with money.

Take a financial inventory. This means sitting down calmly and writing down exactly how much you earn, how much you spend, and how much you owe. It may feel intimidating at first, especially if you've been avoiding looking at your accounts, but it's an act of courage. When you write down the numbers, you're taking control. You're stopping running away and facing reality. And here's the secret: No matter how bad it looks on paper, there's always a way to improve.

Once you have a clear picture of your financial situation, the next step is to change your mindset. Many people view money as something scarce, as if there is never enough. This mindset can cause you to make fear-based financial decisions, such as accepting any credit available or spending on things you don't really need just to feel better for a moment. Instead, try adopting an abundance mindset. This doesn't mean ignoring reality, but rather believing that you can work to improve it. Money doesn't have to be something that controls your life; it can be something you control.

Money is neither good nor bad, it's simply a tool. You don't define your worth as a person by how much you have in your bank account. Often, we carry ideas from the past, things we heard as children, such as "money is the root of all evil" or "rich people are selfish." These beliefs may be sabotaging you without you even realizing it. Ask yourself: What do I really think about money? Where do those ideas come from? Once you identify those beliefs, work on changing them. Money, well managed, can be a positive force in your life.

It's also important to forgive yourself for past financial mistakes. Maybe you spent too much on unnecessary things. Maybe you took out a loan you couldn't pay back. Maybe you trusted someone who led you down the wrong path. Whatever it is, forgive yourself. Guilt won't help you move forward. Instead, learn from those mistakes. Every experience, even the bad ones, is a valuable lesson. The past doesn't define your future. What matters is what you do from now on.

Part of making peace with your finances is learning to be patient with yourself. Don't expect to fix everything in one day. Getting out of debt, saving, and changing your financial habits takes time. There will be days when you feel like you're not making progress, and that's okay. Progress isn't always linear, but every step, no matter how small, counts. The key is to stay focused and committed to your goal.

Also, don't be afraid to ask for help if you need it. Talking about money can be a taboo subject for many people, but it's important to reach out for support. You can talk to a trusted friend, a financial advisor, or even your partner. You don't have to face this alone. Sometimes an outside perspective can help you see solutions you hadn't considered.

Remember that money is a tool to build the life you want. It doesn't have to be a constant source of stress. By making peace with your finances, you're taking a big step toward a freer and more balanced life. It won't be easy at first, but every effort you make will bring you closer to the financial peace of mind you so desire. It doesn't matter where you are now, what matters is where you are willing to go. And that path begins here, with the decision to make peace with your money and use it consciously and wisely.

Creating a Personal Financial Map

Imagine you're in an unfamiliar place and need to get to an important destination. What's the first thing you'd do? You'd probably look for a map or open an app to guide you, right? Well, the same goes for your finances. If you don't know exactly where you are and where you want to go, it's nearly impossible to move forward. Creating a personal financial map is like plotting a route for your money, so that every decision you make brings you closer to your goals. This process not only helps you stay organized, but it also gives you clarity and control over your financial situation.

The first step in creating your financial map is to identify where you are now. This means taking a close look at your income, expenses, debts, and savings. It's like marking your starting point on a map. Sometimes it can be uncomfortable to look at the actual numbers, but you can't improve what you don't understand. Sit down calmly and write everything down on paper or use a spreadsheet. Write down how much you earn each month, whether it's from a regular job, side hustles, or any other source of income. Then, write down what you spend your money on. It's important to be honest and detailed here. Include everything from fixed payments like rent or lease, to small expenses like your morning coffee.

Once you've got a clear idea of where you want to go, it's time to define where you want to go. What do you want to accomplish with your money? Maybe you want to get out of debt, save for an emergency fund, or start investing for the future. These goals are like destinations on your map. It's important to make them specific and realistic. For example, instead of saying "I want to save," say "I want to save $10,000 in a year for emergencies." This gives you a clear objective and allows you to measure your progress.

Now that you know where you are and where you want to go, it's time to map out the route. This is where a budget comes in, which is like the path you will follow to reach your goals. A budget is not a list of restrictions, it is a tool to make sure that every penny you earn has a purpose. Divide your income into categories such as fixed expenses, variable expenses, debt repayment, and savings. For example, if you earn 20,000 a month, you can allocate a percentage to each category, such as 50% for essential expenses, 20% for savings, 20% for debt, and 10% for personal expenses. The key is to be realistic and adjust the budget to your current situation.

But a financial map isn't just about numbers. You also need to anticipate the obstacles in your path. This means thinking about the unexpected, like a medical emergency or an unexpected home repair. That's why one of the first goals of your map should be to build an emergency fund. This fund acts as a cushion that protects you when something unexpected happens. Ideally, you should save three to six months of your basic expenses. If that sounds like a lot, start with a smaller goal, like $5,000 or $10,000. The important thing is to get started.

Another important part of your financial map is assessing your debts. If you have debts, it's critical to include them in your plan. Write down all of your debts, from smallest to largest, along with interest rates and minimum payments. This will help you prioritize which ones to pay off first. A common strategy is the snowball method, where you start by paying off the smallest debt while still making minimum payments on the others. Once you eliminate that debt, you move on to the next one. This method is effective because it gives you small victories that motivate you to keep going.

Additionally, your financial map should include a plan for building healthy money habits. This means being mindful of how you spend and making sure your daily decisions are aligned with your goals. For example, if you know you tend to overspend on impulse purchases, set a limit on those expenses or avoid going to places where you know it's hard to resist temptation. Every small change you make adds up and brings you closer to your goals.

Remember to review your financial map regularly. Life changes, and so do your finances. Maybe you get a raise at work, pay off a debt, or an unexpected expense comes up. Adjust your budget and goals as needed, but always stay focused on the end destination.

Creating a personal financial map isn't something you do once and forget about. It's an ongoing process, but one that gives you a sense of control and direction. In the end, this map will not only help you achieve your goals, but it will also give you peace of mind, because you'll know you're making conscious decisions with your money. And best of all, it will allow you to enjoy the journey more, because you'll know that each step is taking you in the right direction.

The Budget

Talking about budgets often makes many people frown. It can sound boring or complicated, like it involves filling out endless forms or limiting yourself from spending on anything fun. But the reality is that a budget isn't a prison—it's a powerful tool that gives you freedom. When you have a budget, you don't sit in the dark wondering where your money went. Instead, you take control and consciously decide what to spend on and what not to. A budget is simply a plan to make your money work for you, instead of you working to chase it.

The first step to creating a budget is knowing your numbers. This means knowing how much money comes in and how much goes out. Most people have a vague idea of what they make, but they don't always know exactly how much they spend. This is where you need to be honest with yourself. Sit down and review your monthly income, whether it's from your paycheck, side hustles, or any other source. Then, look at your expenses. Include everything: rent or mortgage, utilities, transportation, food, subscriptions, entertainment, and even those little expenses like a coffee or drink that seem insignificant but, when added up, can make a big difference.

Once you're clear on how much you make and how much you spend, it's time to organize your money. A simple and effective formula for dividing up your income is the 50/30/20 rule. According to this rule, 50% of your income should go toward needs, 30% toward wants, and 20% toward savings or paying off debt. For example, if you make $20,000 a month, you'd allocate $10,000 toward essential expenses like housing, utilities, and food; $6,000 toward recreational activities or things that make you happy, like dining out or going to the movies; and $4,000 toward savings or paying off debt. This formula isn't rigid, but it gives you a solid foundation to start with.

A successful budget doesn't just include what you need to spend, but also what you want to achieve. This is where your financial goals come in. Maybe you want to save up for a trip, build an emergency fund, or pay off debt faster. Whatever your goal, allocate a portion of your budget toward achieving it. For example, if your goal is to save $10,000 in six months, you need to set aside at least $1,667 each month. It's important to keep these goals specific and realistic so you don't get frustrated along the way.

Now, not everything is perfect, and you may find at first that your expenses are greater than your income. This can be discouraging, but it’s not the end of the world. This is where budgeting becomes your ally in making adjustments. Review your expenses and decide where you can cut back. Maybe you can cook more at home instead of ordering out, cancel a subscription you don’t use, or cut back on impulse purchases. These small changes may seem insignificant, but they add up quickly and help you free up money for what really matters.

One key aspect of a budget is that it should be flexible. Life is full of unexpected events and not everything will go exactly as you planned. Maybe one month you have an unexpected medical expense or a car repair. This doesn't mean you've failed, just adjust your budget and move on. The key is to stick with the planning habit.

Another practical tip is to use tools to manage your budget. You can use mobile apps, a spreadsheet, or just a notebook. The important thing is that the method is comfortable for you and easy to update. Take a few minutes at least once a week to review how you are doing. Not only does this keep you on track, but it also helps you spot patterns in your spending that you may not have noticed.

Finally, remember that a budget is not a punishment, it's a plan for your peace of mind. It's not about depriving yourself of the things you enjoy, but about making sure you can afford them without regret or stress. It's normal to make mistakes at first, like underestimating certain expenses or overspending on something. The key is to learn from those mistakes and keep improving. In the end, what matters is that you take control of your money and that every penny you earn has a clear purpose.

A budget is like the rudder of a ship. Without it, you can drift along, spending aimlessly and racking up debt without even realizing it. But with a budget, you have a clear direction and can sail toward your financial goals with confidence. No matter how much you make or how much you owe, you can always start budgeting and improve your relationship with money. And best of all, when you see the results, when you manage to save for something important or pay off a debt, you realize that the effort is completely worth it.

The Snowball Effect Strategy

The snowball strategy is one of the most effective and motivating ways to get out of debt. Its name comes from the idea of how a small snowball, as it rolls down a hill, grows and gains momentum. In the same way, this technique helps you build the momentum needed to eliminate all of your debts, starting with the smallest ones and working your way up to the largest ones. It's a simple approach, but incredibly powerful because it combines financial logic with the emotional aspect of feeling progress quickly.

The first step in implementing this strategy is to make a list of all your debts. It doesn't matter if it's a personal loan, a credit card, a debt to a friend, or even a late payment on a utility bill. Everything should be on that list. Then, organize those debts from smallest to largest, based on the total balance you owe on each one. Don't worry about interest at this point, as the snowball effect approach isn't based on cold numbers, but on the motivation you'll feel from seeing quick results.

Once you have your list organized, it's time to focus on the first, smallest debt. This is where the magic begins. Your goal will be to pay off that first debt as quickly as possible. This means that you should put all the extra resources you have toward that debt while still making the minimum payments on the others. You may need to cut back on some temporary expenses, like eating out or unnecessary subscriptions, to free up more money to devote to this purpose. The key is to focus all of your financial energy on that small debt until it is completely eliminated.

Why start with the smallest debt? Because it gives you a quick win, and that sense of accomplishment is incredibly powerful. When you eliminate your first debt, you not only free yourself from a financial burden, but you also prove to yourself that it is possible to dig yourself out of the hole. It's an emotional boost that motivates you to keep going with your other debts. Plus, every time you eliminate a debt, you gain more disposable income since you don't have to keep making monthly payments on that account.

After you pay off the first debt, you take the money you were putting toward that debt and add it to the payment of the next smallest debt. For example, if you were paying $1,000 a month on the first debt and you pay it off, now that $1,000 is added to the minimum payment of the next debt on the list. This means that your ability to pay grows with each debt you eliminate, like a snowball that rolls and gets bigger.

It's important to stay disciplined and not be tempted to use extra money for other expenses. Paying off debt may make you feel like you have more freedom to spend, but remember that that money already has a clear purpose: to help you get out of debt faster. Visualize each payment as a step closer to financial freedom.

Another important aspect of this strategy is that it helps you build a winning mindset. Every debt you eliminate boosts your confidence and gives you more control over your money. You begin to see the financial picture more clearly and realize that with a little effort and commitment, you can achieve any goal you set for yourself. It's not just a strategy to eliminate debt, it's a way to transform your relationship with money.

Some might argue that it would make more sense to focus on the debts with the highest interest first, and that is another valid strategy, known as the avalanche method. However, the snowball effect is based on the positive psychological impact of small victories. Sometimes getting out of debt is not just about numbers, but about staying motivated and not giving up in the process.

Of course, there are times when you might need to adjust your plan. Maybe an unexpected expense comes up, or you find that you need more time to pay off a particular debt. This is okay, as long as you don't lose sight of your main goal. The snowball effect is flexible, and the most important thing is that you keep moving forward, no matter how fast or slow.

Finally, when you get to the last debt on your list, the biggest one, you'll have all your financial power focused on paying it off. By then, you'll likely have more disposable income and a great deal of confidence in your ability to manage your money. Paying off that last debt will be a moment of triumph worth every sacrifice you made along the way.

The snowball effect will not only help you get out of debt, but it will also change the way you view your finances. You will learn to be more conscious of your spending decisions, manage your money with intention, and build a future free of financial burdens. It is a process that takes time and effort, but the rewards are immense. The feeling of freedom and peace that comes from not owing anything to anyone is life-changing. Start today, take the first step, and soon you will see how that small snowball becomes a powerful avalanche that changes your financial life forever.

Breaking the Debt Cycle

Being stuck in a debt cycle is one of the most frustrating and draining experiences anyone can go through. It's like being on a hamster wheel, running non-stop, but never really moving forward. You pay off one debt, but another one pops up. You make an effort to get ahead, but an unexpected expense sinks you again. For many people, this cycle seems endless, but the good news is that it can be broken. It's not easy or immediate, but with a clear plan, commitment, and changes in habits, it's entirely possible to break free from this pattern and take control of your finances.

The first step to breaking the debt cycle is to recognize how it started. Debt doesn't just appear out of nowhere. Often, it's the result of decisions that, at the time, seemed necessary or even harmless. Maybe it was a loan to cover an urgent expense, a credit card that was overused, or financing for something you really wanted but couldn't afford at the time. By identifying the root of the problem, you can begin to take steps to prevent it from happening again. It's an exercise in honesty with yourself, but it's necessary if you want to make lasting change.

Once you understand how you got to where you are, the next step is to stop using debt as a quick fix. This is one of the hardest changes to make, because when you're used to turning to credit cards or loans to get out of trouble, breaking that dependency can be scary. But it's critical. If you keep piling on more debt while trying to get out of the ones you already have, you'll never make any progress. One practical way to start is to commit to not using your credit cards for a while. Put them away somewhere out of reach, or even literally freeze them in a bowl of water in the freezer. The idea is that if you need to use them, it's so deliberate that you have time to think twice.

The next step is to build an emergency fund, even if it's small. Most people fall into the debt cycle because they don't have money saved to cover unexpected expenses. So, instead of turning to a loan or a credit card, they end up accumulating more debt. You don't need to start with a huge amount. Even saving a thousand or two thousand pesos can make a difference. This small financial cushion will be your first line of defense against any unexpected expenses. Every time you receive additional income, such as a bonus or a gift, allocate a portion to this fund. You'll see how, little by little, you feel more prepared to face life without resorting to loans.

Also, it's crucial to learn how to say no. Sometimes the debt cycle perpetuates itself because we want to maintain a lifestyle we can't afford. We want to go out to eat, buy new clothes, go on vacation, or have the latest cell phone model. But if you really want to break the debt cycle, you need to prioritize what really matters. This doesn't mean you have to live a life of deprivation, but it does mean making conscious choices about how you spend your money. Ask yourself if what you're buying is something you need or just something you want at that moment.

Another powerful tool for breaking the debt cycle is learning to negotiate. If you have multiple debts, don't be afraid to talk to your creditors. Often, they are willing to offer you options such as lowering the interest rate, extending the payment term, or even accepting a lump sum payment for an amount less than the total debt. You don't lose anything by trying, and in many cases, it can be the key to freeing yourself from your financial obligations faster. Remember that creditors would rather receive some money than anything else, so use this to your advantage.

Financial education is also essential. Often, the cycle of debt is perpetuated because we don't understand how interest, extra fees, or loan terms work. Take the time to learn the basics of personal finance. Today, there are many free resources online, from videos to articles, that can help you better understand how to manage your money. The more you know, the better equipped you'll be to make smart financial decisions and avoid falling back into the debt trap.

Finally, breaking the debt cycle requires patience. Don't expect immediate results, because getting out of debt takes time. There will be times when you feel like you're not making enough progress, but don't give up. Every step you take, no matter how small, is a step toward financial freedom. Remember that the goal is not just to get out of debt, but also to learn how to live sustainably so you don't fall into the same pattern again.

The process of breaking the debt cycle is challenging, but it is also deeply transformative. Not only will it help you improve your financial situation, but it will also give you a sense of control and empowerment. You will realize that you have the power to change your life, to make different choices, and to build a future where your income works for you, instead of being forever tied down to debt from the past. This change is possible, and it all starts with a commitment to break the cycle and take control of your finances.

Learning to Say 'No'

Saying "no" is one of the most powerful skills, but also one of the hardest to learn when it comes to managing our finances. We live in a world filled with constant invitations to consume. Shiny offers, limited-time discounts, seemingly affordable installments, and daily temptations bombard us relentlessly. However, learning to say "no" doesn't just mean resisting buying something we don't need, but also setting clear boundaries in different areas of our lives that affect our wallets. Saying "no" is an act of self-care and control that can completely transform your relationship with money.

We often avoid saying "no" because we fear the reactions of others. Maybe a friend invites you out to dinner, and even though you know you can't afford the expense, you feel guilty about turning them down. Or maybe a salesperson pressures you into agreeing to an extra service that you clearly don't need, but you feel uncomfortable saying no. In these situations, saying "no" may feel awkward at first, but it's essential to remember that taking care of your finances is your responsibility. No one else will do it for you. When you learn to prioritize your financial goals over the expectations of others, you begin to build a life based on what really matters.

A common mistake is thinking that saying "no" means depriving yourself of everything. It's not about living a life of extreme austerity, but rather being selective about what you choose to spend. Every time you say "no" to something, you're actually saying "yes" to something more important. For example, if you decide not to buy that expensive coffee every day, you're saying "yes" to saving for a vacation or paying down debt. If you decide not to take that loan for a new cell phone you don't need, you're saying "yes" to maintaining your financial stability. Changing this perspective makes every decision feel less like a surrender and more like a step toward your goals.

Saying "no" is also a way to eliminate impulse purchases. How many times have you bought something because it seemed like a good deal or because it made you feel good at the time, only to realize later that you didn't need it? The key is to pause and reflect before you spend. Ask yourself questions like: Do I really need this? Can I afford it without compromising other priorities? How will I feel about it in a week or a month? Taking a few minutes to consider these questions can prevent you from spending money on things that don't add real value to your life.

Learning to say "no" doesn't just apply to your personal expenses, but also to the financial commitments you make for others. Sometimes friends or family members may ask you to help them financially, and while your intentions are good, you must be aware of your own limitations. Helping someone doesn't mean putting your financial stability at risk. It's valid to offer emotional support, guidance, or to look for alternatives together, but you don't have the obligation to go into debt to solve other people's problems. Saying "no" in these situations doesn't make you a bad person; it makes you a responsible person who understands that you can't give what you don't have.

A helpful strategy for learning how to say "no" is to practice clear, kind responses. For example, if someone treats you to something that's out of your budget, you can say, "Thanks for inviting me, but I'm watching my finances right now. Maybe we can do something simpler together." This response not only communicates your decision, but also opens the door to alternative options that don't compromise your goals. Being honest about your priorities is not only valid, but admirable, and can inspire others to do the same.

Another important aspect is learning to say "no" to yourself. We are often our own worst enemies when it comes to overspending. We convince ourselves that we deserve a treat because we work hard, because we are stressed, or because we simply want something. While there is nothing wrong with treating yourself from time to time, it is essential to do so in a planned and conscious way. Ask yourself if that expense really fits into your budget and if it is aligned with your long-term goals. Practicing self-discipline is not easy, but over time it becomes a habit that strengthens your control over money.

Remember, too, that saying "no" is a temporary act. You're not saying "no" forever, you're just postponing certain expenses or decisions until you have the ability to handle them without stress. For example, maybe you can't afford an expensive trip now, but by saying "no" today, you're giving yourself the opportunity to save and fully enjoy it in the future. This approach helps you stay motivated and avoid falling into the trap of believing you'll always have to sacrifice.

Finally, don't forget that every time you say "no," you're reaffirming your commitment to yourself and your financial goals. It's a reminder that you're taking control of your life, instead of letting money control you. At first, it may feel difficult and even uncomfortable, but over time you'll realize that every "no" you say with intention and clarity brings you one step closer to financial freedom. And that freedom is priceless.

The Hidden Danger of Credit Cards

Credit cards seem like an amazing tool. They offer us the possibility of buying something today and paying for it later, almost like they are a friend who is always there to lend us money when we need it. But behind that convenience and ease of use, there is a hidden danger that many people don't see until it's too late. Understanding how credit cards really work and how they can become a financial trap is key to protecting your wallet and your peace of mind.

The main problem with credit cards is that they make us feel like we have more money than we actually do. Every time you swipe your card to pay for something, you're not using money you already have, but borrowed money. And because you don't feel the immediate impact of spending, it's easy to be tempted to buy things you wouldn't have otherwise. It's an expense that seems invisible, but eventually becomes very real when the statement arrives.

Credit cards are also designed to incentivize you to spend more. Rewards programs, accumulating points, and exclusive discounts are all carefully thought-out strategies to get you to use your card more often. While these may sound like attractive benefits, the reality is that most people fail to take advantage of those rewards effectively. Instead, they end up paying much more in interest and fees than they receive in return.

One of the biggest dangers is interest. Many people don't really understand how interest works on credit cards. If you don't pay off your card balance in full at the end of the month, the bank will start charging you interest on the money you owe. And that interest isn't low. In fact, credit card interest rates are often some of the highest compared to other types of debt. This means that what seemed like a small purchase can end up costing you a lot more over time. For example, something you bought for a hundred dollars can end up costing you a hundred and fifty or more if you only make minimum payments month after month.

Minimum payments are another dangerous trap. Many people believe that as long as they make the minimum payment each month, they are managing their credit card well. But this is not true. Minimum payments are designed to lengthen the life of the debt, so that the bank can charge you interest for longer. If you only pay the minimum, it will take years to pay off even a relatively small amount, and you will end up paying much more than you originally owed. It is a strategy that benefits the bank, not you.

Additionally, excessive credit card use can negatively impact your overall financial health. When your credit card debt piles up, it becomes harder to cover your basic expenses and save for your long-term goals. It can also lead to stress and anxiety, as you always have that burden hanging in the back of your mind. This stress can affect not only your finances, but also your emotional well-being and personal relationships.

To make matters worse, credit cards can also put your stability at risk in emergencies. If you use most of your available limit for everyday expenses, you may not have enough room on the card to cover an unexpected expense when you really need it. This can lead you to rely on other, more expensive forms of debt or run out of options at critical times.

So what can you do to avoid falling prey to the hidden dangers of credit cards? First, only use credit cards if you can pay off the balance in full at the end of each month. This allows you to take advantage of the benefits of cards, such as convenience and security, without accruing interest. If you know you can't pay off the balance in full, it's best to avoid using the card altogether and opt for cash or debit instead.

It's also important to set clear limits for yourself. Just because you have a high credit limit doesn't mean you should use it. Define how much you can responsibly spend and stick to that limit, even if the card allows you to spend more. This personal control is crucial to avoid getting into unnecessary debt.

Another tip is to keep track of your spending. Write down every purchase you make with your credit card, just as you would if you were paying cash. This helps you be more aware of how you're using the card and avoid impulse spending. If you prefer digital tools, there are plenty of apps that can help you track your spending and stay within your budget.

Finally, remember that credit cards are not bad per se. They are tools that can be useful if used in a smart and disciplined manner. But it is essential to understand that credit cards are designed to generate profits for banks, not to help you save money. If you are aware of this and manage your cards carefully, you can avoid hidden dangers and keep your finances under control.

The real power of a credit card is in how you choose to use it. By making conscious, responsible choices, you can avoid falling into the traps that ensnare so many people. But if you use them thoughtlessly, credit cards can become a burden that keeps you from your financial goals. The key is to be honest with yourself about your spending habits and take control of your finances before debt takes control of you.

Negotiate and Renegotiate Debts

When you're in debt, one of the most powerful tools you can use to relieve the pressure is negotiation. However, many people don't realize that, contrary to popular belief, you don't always have to accept the original terms of a debt. Often, lenders are willing to negotiate and renegotiate terms to make repayment more affordable, allowing you to get out of debt faster and with less stress.

The first thing you need to understand is that when you're in debt, you're not a helpless victim. You have the right to negotiate. Lenders would rather you pay them, even if it means adjusting the terms, than lose you as a customer and get nothing. Plus, if you can't make payments as per the original terms, you're more likely to reach an agreement if you speak up before the problem escalates into something more serious. If you don't speak up, all the lender will do is keep sending you payment reminders, which will only increase your stress and penalties.

The first step in negotiating or renegotiating debt is to do a clear analysis of your financial situation. Before you reach out to your lenders, it's crucial to have a complete overview of your income, your expenses, and the amount of debt you have. This will give you a solid starting point for discussing a solution that's feasible for you. If you have multiple loans, such as credit cards, personal loans, or auto loans, make sure you know the details of each one: interest rates, outstanding balance, due dates, and penalties. The more prepared you are, the easier it will be to show that you're committed to resolving the situation.

Once you have all this information, the next step is to contact your lenders. You can start with a phone call, but it's often more effective to do so in writing, as there will be a record of the communication. In your message, be honest about your situation. You don't need to go into personal details, but you should clearly explain why you can't continue paying under the original terms. Most of the time, lenders will prefer to work with you to find a solution that will allow you to continue paying. It's important that you show a willingness to make the payment, even if it's on different terms than you initially agreed to. The simple fact that you're seeking a solution demonstrates your commitment, and that may motivate the lender to work with you.

When negotiating, there are several options you can consider, depending on your situation. One of the most common is to request a reduction in the interest rate. If your payments have become unbearable due to high interest, explaining this may lead to the lender being willing to offer you a lower rate. In some cases, if you have a good payment history, even if there are temporary problems, the lender might be willing to make adjustments, as they would rather receive some money than nothing.

Another option is to ask for a deferment or extension of your payment term. If the problem is that you can't make your monthly payments on time, you can ask for an extension, which will allow your payments to be spread out over a longer period. This can help you reduce the amount you have to pay each month, making it more manageable. However, it's important to note that these types of arrangements can result in more interest in the long run, so it's something you should consider carefully.

If you have multiple debts, you can also negotiate an agreement to consolidate them into one payment. This can be helpful if you have multiple debts with different lenders and the interest rates are high. Lenders are often willing to consolidate debts so you can make one monthly payment at a lower interest rate. While this doesn't eliminate the debt, it can make the payments easier to manage.

In some cases, it may be possible to negotiate a waiver, especially if you have a large amount of debt and have been struggling for a long time. A waiver means that the lender agrees to forgive a portion of the debt, reducing the total amount you owe. If you choose this option, it's important to be clear about whether it's the best option for you, as some waiver agreements can affect your credit history. Make sure you understand the consequences before making this decision.

One of the keys to successful negotiation is to be firm but respectful. Negotiation is not a confrontation, it's a conversation. While it's important to stand up for your interests, you should also show a willingness to find a solution that benefits both parties. Sometimes lenders simply need to feel comfortable that you're taking steps to resolve the problem. If you show a willingness to compromise, they're more likely to accept your proposals.

Another important point in the negotiation process is not to be afraid to keep trying if you don't get a favorable response right away. If you can't reach an agreement with your lender or if the conditions they offer don't seem right to you, don't hesitate to seek professional help. There are financial advisory firms and specialized lawyers who can help you negotiate debts. These professionals know the procedures and laws that can benefit your case, which can make the negotiation process easier and more successful.

Finally, it's essential that you stick to the agreed-upon plan once you reach an agreement. If you achieve a new payment date, a lower interest rate, or a longer term, it's crucial that you stick to those new terms. Failing to comply with an agreement can damage your financial reputation and further complicate your situation. If for some reason you can't keep up with the new agreement, let your lenders know as soon as possible. Honesty and ongoing communication are essential to maintaining a positive relationship and preventing debt from growing again.

Negotiating and renegotiating your debts is not an easy process, but it is a powerful tool that will help you regain control of your financial situation. By taking the initiative and working directly with your lenders, you can find workable solutions that will allow you to pay off your debts without feeling like you are drowning. The key is to be proactive, be prepared, and not give up until you find a solution that works for you.

Building an Emergency Fund

An emergency fund is like a financial lifeline. It's money you set aside specifically for unexpected situations, such as a medical emergency, job loss, or an urgent home repair. Having an emergency fund can make the difference between weathering a setback calmly or falling into a cycle of debt to cover unexpected expenses. It's an essential tool for anyone who wants to have a more stable and less stressful financial life.

Building an emergency fund can seem intimidating at first, especially if you're dealing with debt or your budget is already tight. But the good news is that you don't need to start with a huge amount of money. The important thing is to take the first step and commit to growing it over time. Even a small amount can make a big difference down the road. Think of this as a long-term project, not something you have to complete right away.

The first step to building an emergency fund is to set a clear goal. How much do you need to save? Experts typically recommend having three to six months of basic expenses in your emergency fund. This includes things like rent or mortgage, utilities, food, transportation, and any other essential expenses. If this seems unattainable right now, don't worry. You can start with a smaller goal, like saving enough to cover one month of expenses. Once you reach that goal, you can set a new one, and so on.

Once you have a goal in mind, it's time to find ways to start saving. This requires doing an honest analysis of your income and expenses. Examine your current budget and look for areas where you can cut back on expenses. Maybe you can reduce the amount you spend on eating out, cancel subscriptions you don't use, or find cheaper alternatives for certain services. Every dollar you save can go straight into your emergency fund. You may have to make some short-term sacrifices, but remember that this is an investment in your peace of mind and financial security.

Another helpful tip is to treat your emergency fund as a priority, not an option. Many people make the mistake of thinking of saving as something they'll only do if there's money left over at the end of the month. The problem with this approach is that there's rarely any money left over, especially if you don't have a clear plan. Instead, set a set amount that you'll put toward your emergency fund every time you receive an income, whether it's weekly, biweekly, or monthly. You can automate this process by setting up automatic transfers to a separate savings account. This way, the money is saved before you're tempted to spend it.

It's important to choose the right place to keep your emergency fund. This money should be easily accessible in case you need it, but not so accessible that you're tempted to use it for unnecessary expenses. A separate savings account is a good option, especially if it's not linked to your debit card. Some people even choose to open an account at a different bank to reduce the temptation to transfer the money to their main account. The key is to find a balance between accessibility and protection.

As you build your emergency fund, remember that this money is not for impulse purchases or to cover expenses you may have planned ahead of time. For example, you shouldn't use your emergency fund to buy birthday presents or pay for a vacation. This money is reserved only for unexpected and urgent situations. For other goals, such as vacations or large purchases, you can create a separate savings fund.

One of the best ways to grow your emergency fund is to look for additional ways to generate income. This could mean taking on a side job, selling things you no longer need, or monetizing a hobby. Every extra peso you earn can speed up the process and help you reach your goal faster. While this takes effort, think about how you'll feel when you have that financial cushion ready to protect you in case of any emergency.

You're bound to hit bumps along the way. Maybe you'll have a rough month where you can't save as much as you'd like, or even a month where you have to use part of your fund for a real emergency. Don't get discouraged. The important thing is to get back on track as soon as possible and keep saving. Building an emergency fund isn't a perfect process, but every little bit counts.

Finally, once you've reached your goal, don't forget to review it periodically. Your financial needs may change over time, especially if your work, family, or housing situation evolves. You may find that you need to increase your emergency fund to cover higher expenses or to adapt to new risks. Keeping this fund up to date is an important part of your financial strategy.

Building an emergency fund takes patience, discipline, and commitment, but the payoff is worth it. Having that money set aside will give you a sense of security and control that is hard to measure. Knowing that you can face the unexpected without relying on credit cards or loans will be a huge relief. This fund not only protects your finances, but also your emotional well-being, allowing you to live with less stress and more confidence in the future.

Avoiding Credit Traps

Credit can seem like the magic solution to many of our financial problems. When we need money fast, it's tempting to accept any offer that promises to cover our needs immediately. However, not all credits are created equal, and some can become real traps that sink us deeper into debt instead of helping us get out of it. Learning to identify and avoid these trap credits is an essential skill to protect our finances and our peace of mind.

Loan scams are often presented as easy and accessible options, but behind the attractive promises there are conditions that can be very unfavorable. These loans often have extremely high interest rates, hidden fees, or terms that are not always clearly explained. At first, they may seem like a viable solution, but in the long run, they end up costing you much more than they are worth. It is important to remember that the companies that offer these loans are not thinking about your well-being; their main goal is to maximize their profits, even if that means taking advantage of your urgency or lack of information.

One of the first signs of a credit trap is a disproportionately high interest rate. For example, many credit cards or quick personal loans have interest rates that can exceed 50 percent annually. This means that if you take out a small loan, you'll end up paying much more in interest than the original amount. Although the monthly payments may seem manageable, they're often designed to keep you paying for years, without significantly reducing the principal balance. This creates a feeling of stagnation that can be frustrating and difficult to overcome.

Another common aspect of loan scams is hidden fees. Often, these charges are not clearly explained when you sign the contract. They can include credit opening costs, prepayment penalties, or even insurance you did not request. These fees increase the total cost of the loan and make it more difficult to pay off. Before accepting any offer, it is crucial to read the terms and conditions carefully. If something is not clear, ask for clarification or seek advice before committing.

Some companies also use aggressive marketing tactics to convince you that you need a loan that you could actually avoid. Phrases like “no requirements,” “instant approval,” or “without checking your credit history” are attractive, but they are often a warning sign. These loans are designed for people who may be desperate or have few options, and companies know this. That's why it's essential to take the time to evaluate whether you really need that money and whether you can pay it back without compromising your finances.

A good rule of thumb to avoid falling into credit traps is to never make impulsive decisions. If you are considering a loan, take at least 24 hours to think it over calmly. Research other options and compare them. Ask yourself if the loan is really necessary or if you can resolve your situation in another way. Many times, the pressure of immediacy leads us to make decisions that we regret later.

It's also important to understand the difference between necessary and unnecessary credit. Necessary credit might be credit you use for a medical emergency or to repair something essential, like your car or home's electrical system. Unnecessary credit, on the other hand, is credit you use to buy things that aren't urgent or that you could save up for later, like a new phone or a vacation. Learning to distinguish between these types of needs can help you avoid going into debt for no reason.

If you decide that a loan is your best option, make sure you choose one with fair terms. Look for low interest rates and reasonable terms that will allow you to repay without putting your financial stability at risk. Also, check the reputation of the entity offering the loan. Research reviews and experiences from other customers to make sure it is a trustworthy company. Never sign a contract without fully understanding the conditions, and don't be afraid to ask questions.

Another key strategy to avoid loan traps is to strengthen your emergency fund and your savings. The more prepared you are to face unexpected events, the less you will depend on credit to solve them. Although building an emergency fund takes time, it is one of the best ways to protect yourself from financial traps. Every peso you save now is one peso less you will have to borrow in the future.

Remember that credit is not inherently bad. It can be a useful tool when used responsibly and with full knowledge of its terms. However, it is crucial to maintain a critical attitude and always be on the lookout for offers that seem too good to be true. If something seems easy and quick, there is probably a hidden cost that you need to uncover before you commit.

Financial education is your best defense against loan scams. The more you know about how loans, interest rates, and fees work, the easier it will be to spot deceptive offers. Investing time in learning about these topics can save you a lot of money and stress in the future. Always remember that debt should not be a burden that drags you down, but rather a tool that, if absolutely necessary, you should handle with care and wisdom.

The Psychology of Money

Money, beyond being a means of exchange, has a profound impact on our minds and emotions. The relationship we have with money is not only shaped by the figures that appear in our bank account, but by the beliefs, experiences and habits we have accumulated throughout our lives. Understanding the psychology of money is essential to managing it intelligently and preventing it from controlling our lives.

From a young age, we absorb messages about money from those around us, especially our families. If you grew up in a home where money was always a topic of concern, you may associate finances with stress and anxiety. On the other hand, if your environment talked about money as something abundant and easy to get, you likely have a more relaxed relationship with it. These early perceptions become deeply ingrained beliefs that affect how we spend, save, or even how we feel about it.

One of the most common beliefs is that money is either the root of all problems or the magic solution to all of them. Both extremes are dangerous. If you believe that money is inherently bad, you might unconsciously sabotage your own opportunities to obtain it. On the other hand, if you think that money will solve all of your problems, you might pursue it at the expense of your happiness and well-being. The key is to view it as a neutral tool: neither good nor bad, simply a means to achieve specific goals.

Money is also deeply connected to our emotions. Many people spend money to fill emotional voids or as a way to escape stress. It's common to see someone buy things they don't need simply because they're going through a bad time. While that purchase may provide a momentary sense of satisfaction, it doesn't solve the underlying problem and often creates a new one: unnecessary debt. Learning to identify when you're using money as an emotional palliative is a crucial step toward a healthier relationship with your finances.

Another psychological aspect of money is how it affects us socially. We live in a society that, in many cases, measures success based on material goods. This can lead us to spend more than we have to maintain an image that doesn’t necessarily reflect our reality. Social media, for example, exacerbates this pressure by constantly showing us images of seemingly perfect lives filled with luxuries. It's important to remember that appearances don't always tell the whole story, and that many of those people could be struggling with debt or financial insecurities behind the scenes.

A common misconception is that if only you had more money, all your problems would disappear. While having financial stability can alleviate many worries, it does not automatically guarantee happiness. Some people with modest incomes lead full and happy lives, while others with large fortunes experience high levels of stress and loneliness. This shows that personal satisfaction comes more from how we manage our finances and our lives in general, than from the exact amount we earn.

To change your relationship with money, it's crucial to start by analyzing your current financial habits and the emotions associated with them. Ask yourself why you spend on certain things or why you avoid facing your debts. This type of introspection can reveal patterns you hadn't noticed before that could be hindering your progress. Once you understand these patterns, you can work on replacing them with healthier habits.

Financial education also plays a crucial role in money psychology. Many of the poor decisions we make with our finances stem from a lack of knowledge. Understanding basic concepts like interest rates, budgeting, and long-term planning can transform your relationship with money and give you a sense of control you may never have experienced before.

A helpful exercise is to define what money means to you. Is it security, freedom, power, or something else entirely? This reflection can help you align your financial goals with your personal values. For example, if money represents security to you, working on building an emergency fund may be a priority. If it represents freedom, reducing your debt can give you the peace of mind you need to pursue your dreams.

Money also teaches us about the importance of balance. Spending everything you earn without thinking about the future can lead to a financial crisis, but saving every penny and not allowing yourself to enjoy life can also lead to frustration and stress. Finding a middle ground, where you can cover your needs, save for the future and treat yourself, is essential to maintaining a healthy relationship with your finances.

Finally, remember that money psychology isn't just about numbers or strategies, but about how you feel and think about your financial resources. Changing your mindset toward money doesn't happen overnight, but with patience and determination you can transform the way you handle your finances and ultimately your quality of life. Money shouldn't be a burden or an end in itself, but rather a tool you use to build the life you want.

Educating the Family About Money

Talking about money as a family may seem awkward or unnecessary, but it is one of the most important topics we can share with our loved ones. Educating your family about money not only helps prevent financial mistakes, but it also strengthens family ties by creating a culture of support and understanding. Although many people avoid these topics for fear of arguments or because they think their children won't understand, the truth is that it is never too early or too late to start.

The first step in educating your family about money is being honest about your own relationship with finances. This doesn't mean sharing every detail of your bank account, but simply explaining how you manage your money, the lessons you've learned, and the mistakes you've made. This kind of transparency can be a great lesson for family members, especially children, who tend to learn by watching. If they see you budgeting, saving, or avoiding impulse spending, they'll be more inclined to adopt those habits in their own lives.

It's crucial to tailor the conversation to each family member's level of understanding.

With young children, for example, you can start by teaching them basic concepts like the value of money and the difference between wants and needs. Something as simple as giving them a piggy bank and encouraging them to save for something they really want can be a powerful lesson. Explaining to them that money doesn't grow on trees, but that with patience and effort they can achieve their goals, gives them a valuable perspective from an early age.

With teens, conversations can become more specific and practical. This is a good time to talk about the importance of a budget, how credit cards and interest work, and why saving for emergencies is vital. You can also teach them about the real cost of things, from college tuition to the basic expenses of living on their own. Giving them the opportunity to manage a small amount of money, like their allowance or money they earn from a part-time job, is a great way for them to practice financial responsibility in a safe environment.

Involving your partner in financial education is also key. Often, couples avoid talking about money because it can be a topic of conflict. However, when you are both aligned on your financial goals, it is easier to work together to achieve them. Talk openly about your income, debt, priorities, and dreams. Decide together how to handle shared expenses and how to approach long-term goals, such as saving for a home, children's education, or retirement. Clear and regular communication about money can prevent misunderstandings and strengthen the relationship.

An important aspect of educating your family about money is teaching them to value things. We live in a society where overconsumption is the norm, and we often buy things we don't need simply because they're trendy or because we want to impress others. Teaching your family to distinguish between what really brings them value and what is simply an unnecessary expense can make a big difference in their financial habits. This doesn't mean depriving yourself of everything, but learning to spend consciously on what really matters.

It's also important to address the topic of financial mistakes. We all make them at some point, and it's critical for the family to understand that mistakes aren't the end of the world, but rather opportunities to learn. Share your own experiences and how you overcame them. If a family member is facing financial problems, instead of judging them, offer support and guidance. This creates an environment where everyone feels comfortable talking about money, making education and learning easier.

Another key point is to set family financial goals. This can be something as big as saving for a vacation or something simpler like cutting back on eating out. Involve everyone in the process, from the youngest to the adults. Not only does this teach them the importance of planning and working together, but it also reinforces a sense of unity and purpose within the family.

Finally, take advantage of the resources available to make financial education easier. There are books, games, apps, and videos designed specifically to teach about money in a fun and accessible way.

Incorporating these resources into your family routine can make learning more interactive and less intimidating. Plus, showing that you, too, are willing to continue learning about finances reinforces the message that financial education is an ongoing process.

Educating your family about money isn't something that happens overnight, but the results are worth it. A family that understands and respects the value of money is better prepared to face financial challenges, make smart decisions, and build a more stable and happy future. In the end, it's not just about the numbers, but about the values and habits you'll pass on to the next generation. By teaching them about money, you're also giving them tools to lead a fuller, more meaningful life.

The Importance of Generating Additional Income

In everyday life, we rely on income to meet our needs and, hopefully, to treat ourselves to a few things. However, we often live on the edge of what we earn, hoping that an unexpected expense doesn't come up and break our budget. Generating additional income may seem like something optional or only necessary in emergencies, but the truth is that it is a practice that can change our financial stability and our outlook for the future. More income means more options, more security, and, above all, more freedom.

The idea of generating additional income can sound overwhelming at first. You may think that you don't have time, that you're already too busy with your main job, or that you don't have skills that you can monetize. But the truth is, with a little creativity and determination, there are many ways to create new sources of income without compromising your current life too much. It's not about working harder, but about working smarter, using your talents, passions, and available resources.

One of the most important reasons to generate extra income is to build a financial cushion. Living paycheck to paycheck can be stressful, especially if every time an unexpected expense comes along, such as a car repair or a medical emergency, you feel like your world is falling apart. Extra income allows you to save faster and feel a greater sense of control over your life. A solid nest egg is not only reassuring, but it also gives you the ability to weather any unexpected events without going into debt.

Another key benefit is the ability to reduce debt. If you have loans, credit cards, or other financial obligations, additional income can speed up the payoff process. Imagine what your life would be like without the burden of debt. Every additional dollar you earn can go straight toward eliminating those outstanding balances, bringing you closer to financial freedom and saving you money on interest in the long run.

Plus, extra income can be the key to achieving personal goals that might otherwise seem impossible. Maybe you've always wanted to travel, buy a home, invest in your education, or even start your own business. With your primary income barely enough to cover basic expenses, those goals may seem far away. But with an extra source of income, every effort brings you a little closer to what you truly want.

It's important to note that you don't need to reinvent the wheel to generate additional income. It can be as simple as offering services or products related to what you already do well. If you have cooking skills, you could sell meals from home. If you're good with technology, you could help others repair their devices or teach them how to use them. If you have a passion for writing, creating online content or publishing an e-book can be a profitable option. The key is to identify what you love to do and how you can bring value to other people with it.

Another common way to earn extra income is by taking advantage of digital platforms. Nowadays, with the ease of social media and marketplaces, you can sell used products, create online courses, start a YouTube channel, or even rent out a room in your home. These opportunities don't always require a large initial investment and can fit into your schedule and lifestyle.

The digital world has democratized income-generating opportunities, and anyone with internet access can find their niche.

If you prefer something more traditional, you can also consider part-time jobs or freelance projects. Many companies look for people who can help out on an hourly basis or on specific tasks, allowing you to earn extra money without making a long-term commitment. This can be especially helpful if you have a talent or professional experience that can be applied to different areas.

One of the biggest benefits of having extra income is peace of mind. Knowing that you're not solely dependent on one main income gives you a greater sense of security. This is especially relevant during times of economic or job uncertainty. If you lose your main job or face a reduction in income, that extra source can be your lifeline while you get back on your feet.

It's also important to mention that extra income doesn't have to be permanent. It can be something temporary to reach a specific goal, like paying off debt or saving for a project. But once you experience the relief and possibilities that come with having extra money, you'll likely want to keep looking for ways to generate more income, simply because you realize how helpful it can be.

However, generating additional income requires discipline and commitment. Sometimes it means sacrificing a little free time or changing the way you manage your day. But the long-term benefits far outweigh the temporary inconvenience. Plus, you'll often find that the extra work doesn't feel like a burden if you truly enjoy what you're doing. That's another reason to choose something you're passionate about and comfortable doing.

Ultimately, earning extra income not only improves your financial situation, but it also gives you the opportunity to learn, grow, and explore new possibilities. It's a way to take control of your future, build the life you want, and eliminate the stress of always living on the edge. No matter where you start, the important thing is to take the first step and be consistent. Over time, that little extra effort can turn into a big positive change for you and your family.

Celebrating Financial Achievements

When we talk about finances, we tend to focus on goals, strategies, and sacrifices. However, there is one crucial aspect that we often overlook: the importance of celebrating financial achievements. Every time you reach a financial goal, no matter how small, you are taking a step toward a more stable and fulfilling life, and that progress deserves to be recognized. Celebrating is not only rewarding, but it also reinforces your motivation and helps you stay focused on the path to your larger goals.

Celebrating doesn't necessarily mean spending money recklessly or derailing your progress. It's about recognizing your effort, valuing your progress, and allowing yourself to enjoy the result of your discipline. Sometimes managing to save a specific amount, paying off a significant debt, or staying within your budget for several consecutive months may seem like a small step in the grand scheme of things, but they are actually significant milestones that demonstrate your commitment and determination. Every financial achievement counts, and it's essential to learn to value them.

An easy way to celebrate is to treat yourself to a small treat that doesn't put a financial strain on your finances. It can be something as basic as a special meal at home, a trip to the movies, or an item you've been wanting for a while but that fits within your budget. The key is to enjoy yourself without feeling guilty, remembering that this celebration is a reward for the effort you've put into improving your financial situation. These moments of celebration aren't a setback, but rather a way to reaffirm your ability to balance responsibility with enjoyment.

It's also important to involve your family or loved ones in these celebrations, especially if they've been a part of your financial journey. Maybe your kids participated in the effort by understanding the importance of saving or your partner was by your side supporting you as you worked together toward a goal. Celebrating together strengthens bonds and teaches everyone that financial progress is not only important, but also something worth recognizing and sharing.

Another powerful way to celebrate is to reflect on your progress. Take a moment to look back and remember where you were when you started. It's easy to forget the progress we've made when we're constantly focused on what's left to accomplish. Maybe you were once saddled with debt and now you're closer to financial freedom. Maybe you once struggled to save, but now you have an emergency fund slowly growing. These accomplishments don't happen by accident; they're a direct result of your hard work and dedication.

Documenting your accomplishments can also be a motivating way to celebrate them. You can keep a financial journal where you record each goal you achieve and how you felt when you accomplished it. Over time, this record becomes tangible proof of your ability to meet your goals and overcome obstacles. You can even include photos or thank-you notes to yourself to further reinforce the feeling of success.

Don't underestimate the power of sharing your achievements with people you trust. Talking about your financial progress with close friends or family can be a source of pride and a way to inspire others. Maybe someone in your circle needs to hear that it's possible to get ahead with hard work and discipline, and your story can be the push they need to start their own journey toward financial stability. Celebrating not only benefits you, but can also create a positive effect on those around you.

It's also crucial to avoid falling into the trap of minimizing your achievements. Sometimes we think our goals are too small to be worth celebrating, especially when we compare them to other people's goals. But remember that each person has their own path and their own challenges. What may seem easy to someone else may have required extraordinary effort for you. Don't compare yourself to others; celebrate what you've achieved from where you started and under your own circumstances.

Ultimately, celebrating your financial achievements is not just about enjoying the moment, but also about using that moment to reaffirm your goals for the future. Every success is a reminder that you are capable of achieving what you set out to do, and every celebration should be a platform that propels you toward the next challenge. After all, the financial journey doesn't end with an achievement; it's a continuous process of learning, growing, and improving.

Allow yourself to feel proud of what you have accomplished. Celebrate every step that brings you closer to the life you want. Recognize that every responsible decision, every sacrifice, and every effort was worth it. In the end, the real reward is not just what you accomplished, but who you became by doing it. Celebrating is not a luxury; it is a necessity to maintain enthusiasm and focus on your path to financial success.

A Debt-Free Future

Imagine for a moment what your life would be like if you didn't have to worry about debt. Think of the freedom of not having to wait every month for a stack of bills or automatic payments that take up a large portion of your income. Visualize the peace of mind of knowing that the money you earn is completely yours, ready to be used on what really matters to you. That debt-free future isn't a distant dream or something reserved only for a lucky few. It's something you can build with effort, planning, and a dose of commitment.

The first key to achieving a debt-free future is to understand that it's not just about eliminating the debts you have today, but also about changing the way you view money and the decisions you make with it. Often, debt is the result of disorganized financial habits or impulses we haven't learned to control. That's why getting out of debt is not only a process of payment, but also a process of personal transformation. To live debt-free, you need to let go of the idea that you need things right now, even if that means going into debt to get them.

A critical step to starting this journey is to stop taking on new debt while you work on eliminating old debt. If you keep charging up your credit cards or taking out new loans, it will be nearly impossible to get ahead. This may require tough decisions, like stopping using credit cards altogether or learning to live on a strict budget. But these temporary sacrifices serve a great purpose: They are setting you up for a calmer, more fulfilling life.

To work toward a debt-free future, you need to have a clear plan. It's not enough to pay what you can when you can; you need a solid strategy that allows you to attack your debts efficiently. One effective option is the debt snowball method, where you order your debts from smallest to largest based on balance and pay off the smallest ones first, while making the minimum payments on the others. Each time you eliminate a debt, you're freed from one burden and can focus on the next. This method not only works mathematically, but it also has a positive emotional impact. Each small victory gives you the momentum you need to keep going.

However, it's not enough to pay off existing debt. You also need to create a buffer to protect you from falling back into debt. An important part of that buffer is an emergency fund. Debt often arises from unexpected expenses, such as car repairs or medical emergencies. If you have a well-established emergency fund, you can cover these expenses without turning to loans or credit cards. Start with a small goal, such as saving a thousand dollars, and then work toward having at least three to six months of basic expenses covered.

Another important aspect of building a debt-free future is learning to manage temptations. We live in a society that constantly bombards us with advertising and messages telling us that we need more things to be happy. Learning to say no to these temptations is not easy, but it is essential. Always ask yourself if what you want to buy is a necessity or just an impulsive desire. If you can't pay for it in cash, don't buy it. This simple principle can save you a lot of headaches in the future.

In addition to avoiding new debt, it's important to look for ways to increase your income. This doesn't necessarily mean getting a second job, although that can be an option in some cases. It can also mean selling things you no longer need, looking for business opportunities, learning new skills that will earn you more money, or investing in something that will generate passive income for you in the long term. Having an additional income stream can greatly accelerate your path to financial freedom.

Once you're out of debt, the key is to stay out of it. This means continuing to live on a budget, saving regularly, and being careful about the financial decisions you make. It can be tempting to think that once you're out of debt, you can just sit back and go back to spending like you did before. But that's the quickest way to get back to square one. Instead, enjoy the freedom of not owing anyone money and use that freedom to build the life you truly want.

Living debt-free also allows you to be more generous. When you don't have debts eating up every penny of your income, you can help others, whether through donations, supporting a friend or family member in need, or investing in causes you care about. That's one of the biggest rewards of living debt-free: the ability to use your money to make a positive difference in the world.

Finally, remember that a debt-free future is not only a financial achievement, but also a way to take care of your emotional and mental well-being. Debt is a constant source of stress and worry for many people. Being debt-free will not only give you more money to spend or save, but also more peace of mind and happiness. At the end of the day, that peace of mind is worth more than anything you could have bought with a credit card.

Building a debt-free future takes time, effort, and sacrifice, but it is an achievable goal. More importantly, it is a goal that will change your life for the better. Don't let debt define your future. Take control of your finances, make a plan, and work on it with determination. The day you finally become debt-free will be the beginning of a new stage, one in which money works for you and not the other way around.